PIANO • VOCAL • GUITAR

ERIC CLAPTON HAPPY XMAS

ISBN: 978-1-5400-3744-2

Visit Hal Leonard Online at
www.halleonard.com

Contact Us:
Hal Leonard
7777 West Bluemound Road
Milwaukee, WI 53213
Email: info@halleonard.com

In Europe contact:
Hal Leonard Europe Limited
42 Wigmore Street
Marylebone, London, W1U 2RN
Email: info@halleonardeurope.com

In Australia contact:
Hal Leonard Australia Pty. Ltd.
4 Lentara Court
Cheltenham, Victoria, 3192 Australia
Email: info@halleonard.com.au

WHITE CHRISTMAS
from the Motion Picture Irving Berlin's HOLIDAY INN

Words and Music by
IRVING BERLIN

all your Christ - mas - es _____ be white.

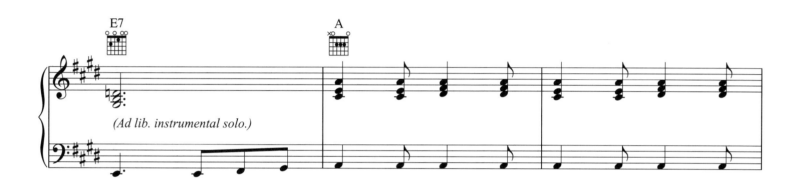

(Ad lib. instrumental solo.)

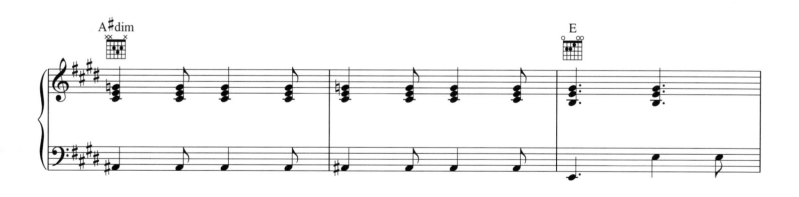

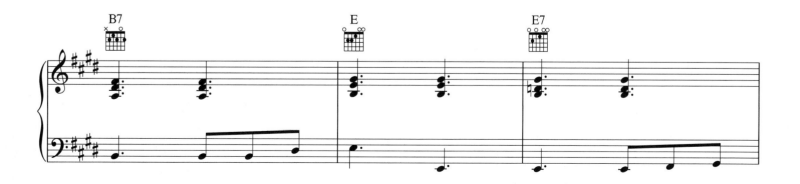

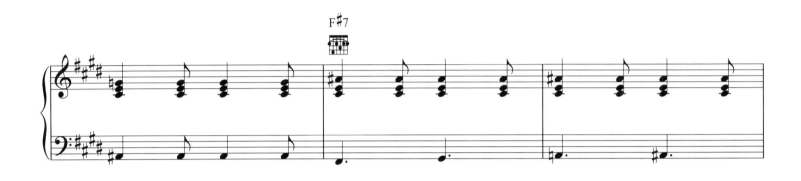

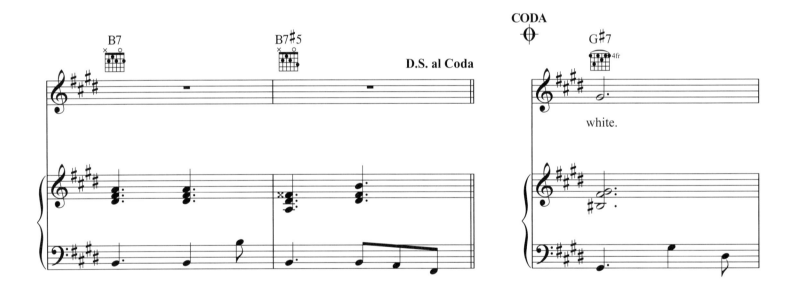

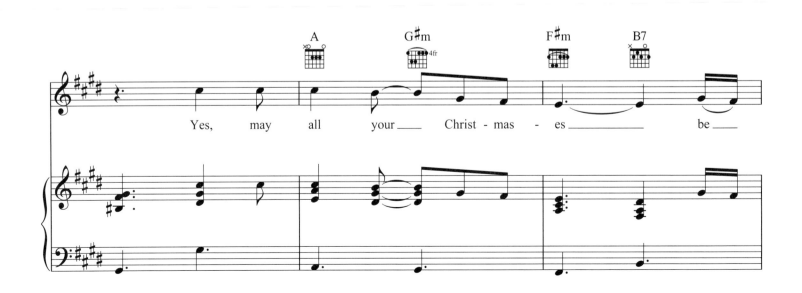

white. _____ (Ad lib. solo fills)

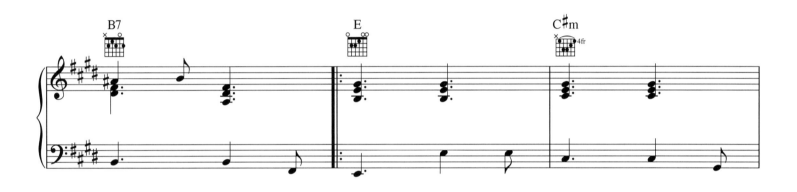

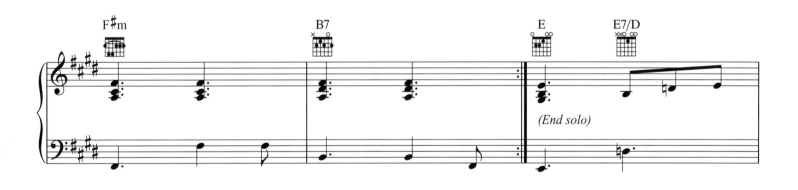

(End solo)

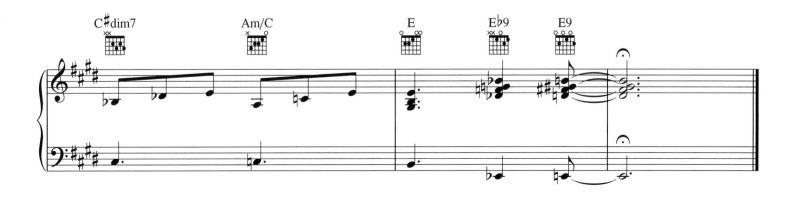

AWAY IN A MANGER
(Once in Royal David's City)

Traditional
Arranged by ERIC CLAPTON
and SIMON CLIMIE

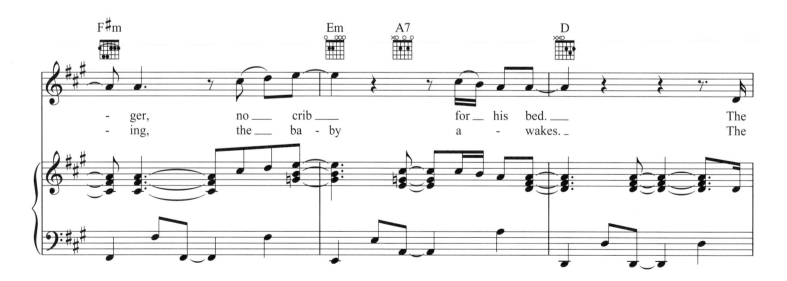

FOR LOVE ON CHRISTMAS DAY

Words and Music by ERIC CLAPTON,
SIMON CLIMIE and DENNIS MORGAN

Snow is on the side - walk,
it's cold in - side my heart. I look ___ up and I won - der have I lost my guid - ing star?

for love on Christ - mas day.

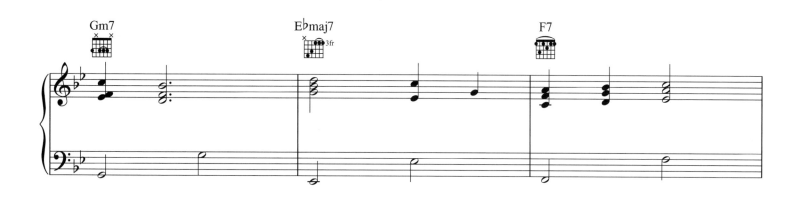

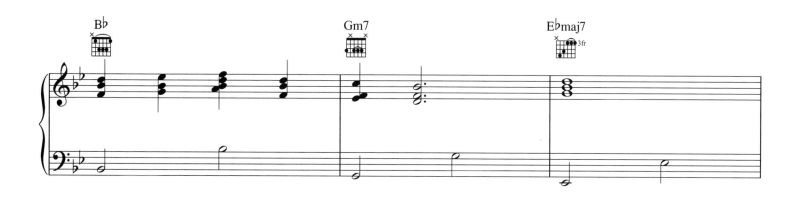

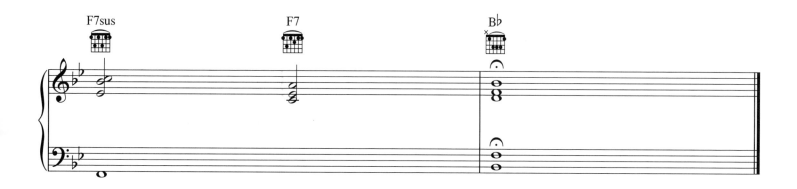

EVERYDAY WILL BE LIKE A HOLIDAY

Words and Music by WILLIAM BELL
and BOOKER JONES

Ev - 'ry day ___ will be like ___ a hol - i - day when my ba - by, when my ba - by comes ___ home.

HOME FOR THE HOLIDAYS

Words and Music by ANTHONY HAMILTON
and KELVIN WOOTEN

I'll be home for the hol - i - days. ___ Think - ing I'd stay a - way, ___

I can't wait to see your smil - ing face. ___ Ba - by, I'm on my way, ___

so hold on. _____

Repeat and Fade

Optional Ending

rit.

CHRISTMAS TEARS

Words and Music by SONNY THOMPSON
and ROBERT WILSON

but on the in - side, cry - in' Christ - mas tears.

Well, you've been gone _____ for a long, _

(2.) Guitar solo ad lib. to end

_____ long time; _ but it's Christ - mas: I can't keep you

off of my mind. Yes, you've been gone for a

long,   lone - ly   years, __   I   can't help but   cry   Christ - mas

tears.

JINGLE BELLS
(In Memory of Avicii)

Traditional
Arranged by ERIC CLAPTON,
SIMON CLIMIE, SALIF KEITA
and MANFILA KANTE

CHRISTMAS IN MY HOME TOWN

Words and Music by SONNY JAMES
and JOHN SKYE

IT'S CHRISTMAS

Words and Music by ANTHONY HAMILTON,
BRANDON DAVIS and KELVIN WOOTEN

Sleigh bells _ out in the at - mos - phere, keep - ing the spir - it a - live. _

_ Sug - ar Belle's _ out on the shop - ping street,

SENTIMENTAL MOMENTS

from the Paramount Major Motion Picture WE'RE NO ANGELS

Words and Music by RALPH FREED
and FREDERICK HOLLANDER

LONESOME CHRISTMAS

Words and Music by
LLOYD GLENN

MERRY CHRISTMAS, BABY

Words and Music by LOU BAXTER
and JOHNNY MOORE

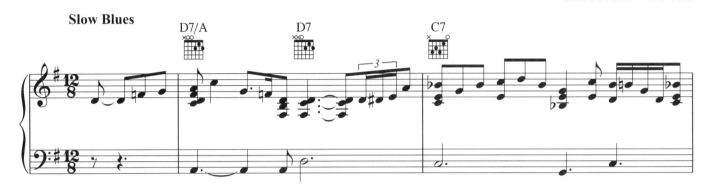

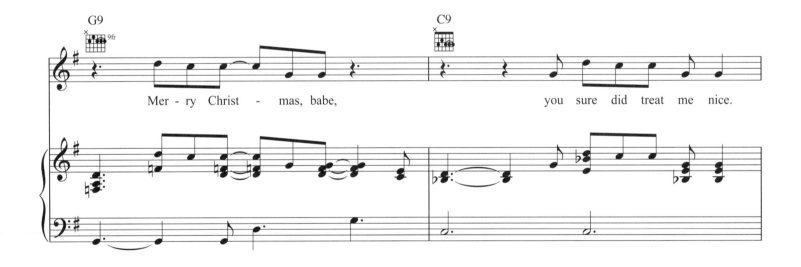

Mer - ry Christ - mas, babe, you sure did treat me nice.

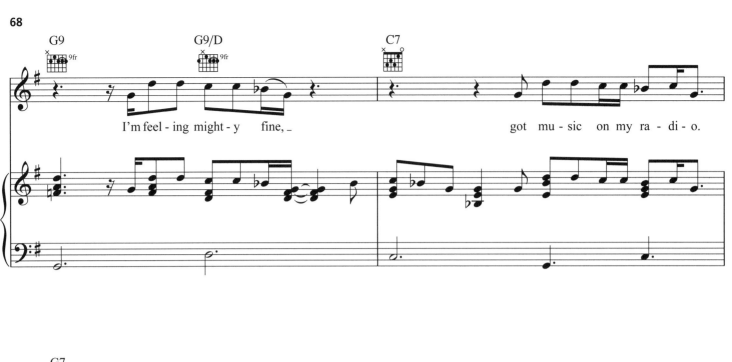

I'm feel - ing might - y fine, _ got mu - sic on my ra - di - o.

Feel - ing might - y fine, _ got good mu - sic on my ra - di - o.

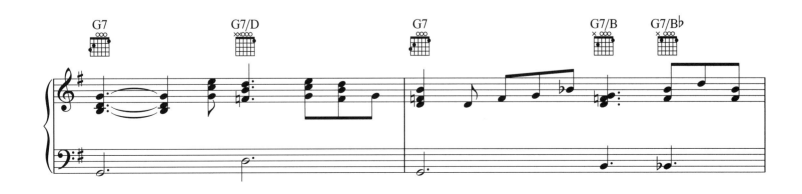

Want to hug and kiss you   un - der - neath the mis - tle - toe.

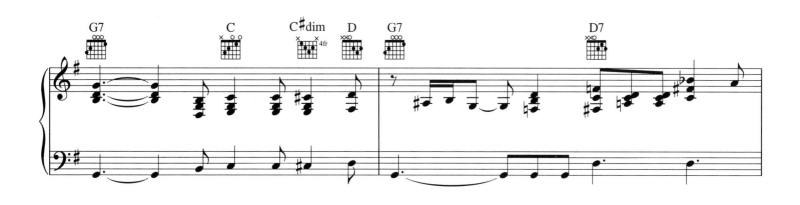

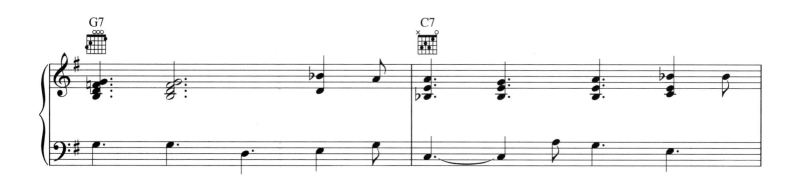

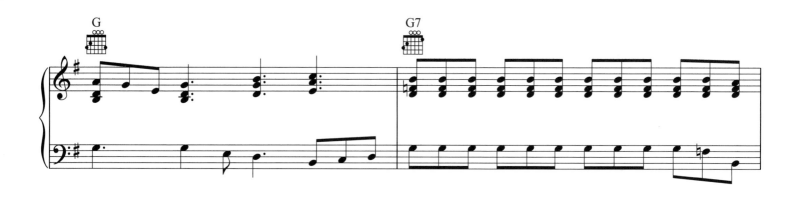

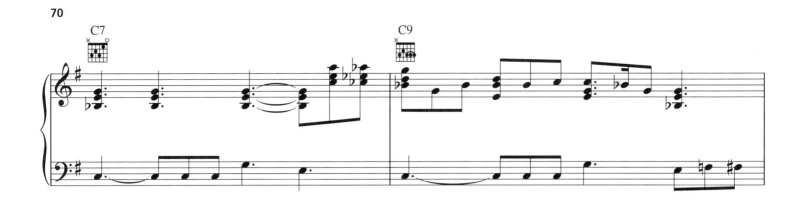

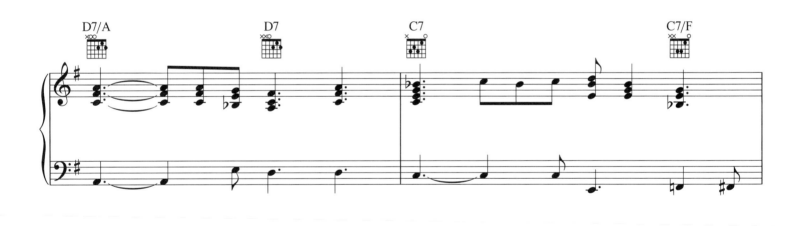

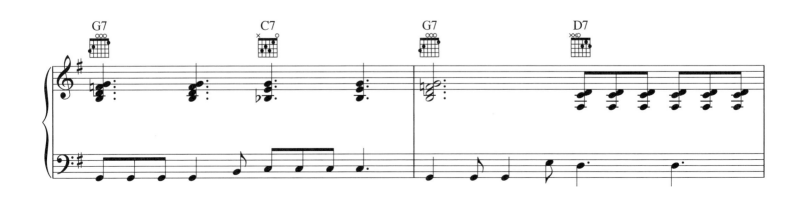

You know I love you, ba - by, and I'm hap-py as a man can be.

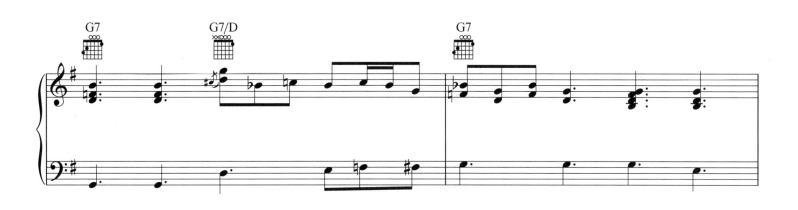

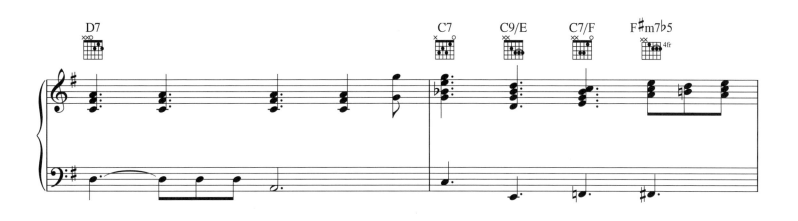

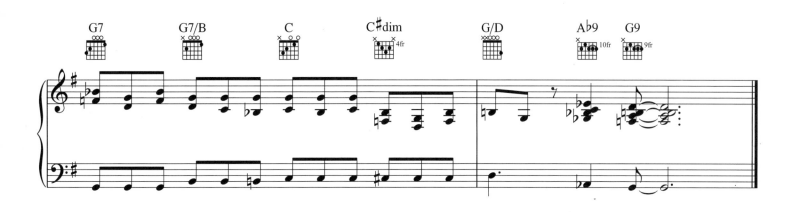

HAVE YOURSELF A MERRY LITTLE CHRISTMAS

from MEET ME IN ST. LOUIS

Words and Music by HUGH MARTIN
and RALPH BLANE

Slow Ballad

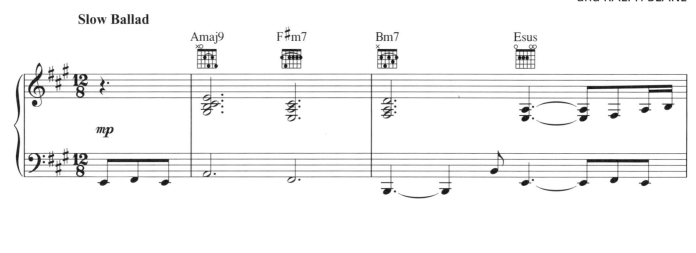

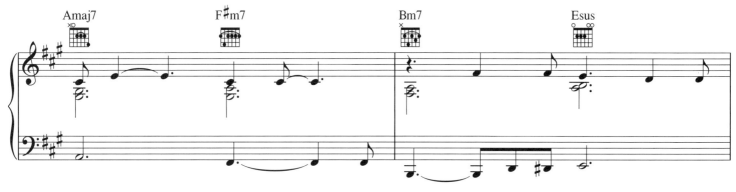

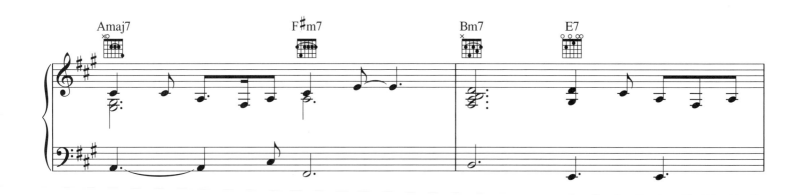

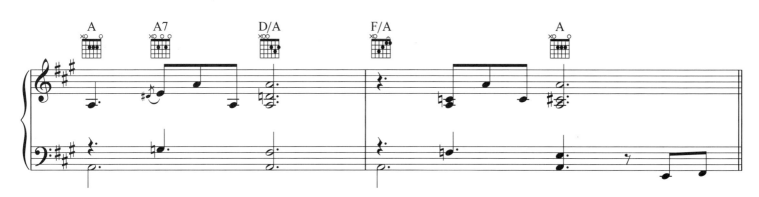

YOU ALWAYS HURT
THE ONE YOU LOVE

Words and Music by ALLAN ROBERTS
and DORIS FISHER

Moderate Swing

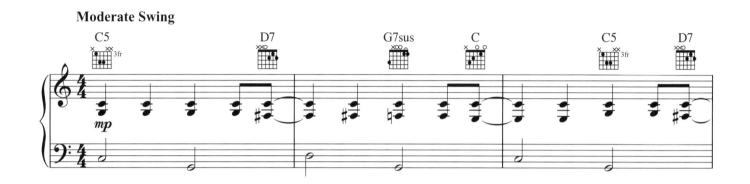

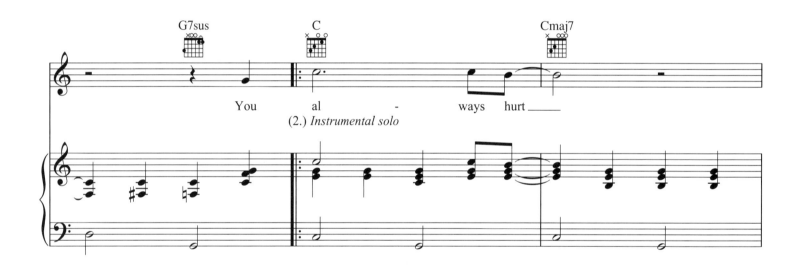

You al - ways hurt _____
(2.) *Instrumental solo*

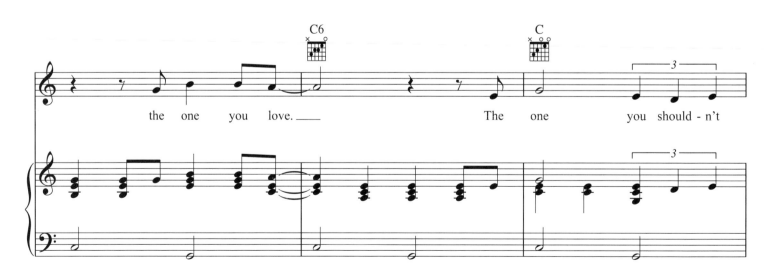

the one you love. _____ The one you should - n't

most of all. _____

You

A LITTLE BIT OF CHRISTMAS LOVE

Words and Music by
ROSCOE GORDON

Moderate Rock

SILENT NIGHT

Traditional
Arranged by ERIC CLAPTON,
WALT RICHMOND and SIMON CLIMIE